SYSTEMS OF GOVERNMENT
MONARCHY

Nathaniel Harris

WORLD ALMANAC® LIBRARY

Please visit our web site at: www.worldalmanaclibrary.com
For a free color catalog describing World Almanac® Library's list of high-quality books
and multimedia programs, call 1-800-848-2928 (USA) or 1-800-387-3178 (Canada).
World Almanac® Library's fax: (414) 332-3567.

Library of Congress Cataloging-in-Publication Data

Harris, Nathaniel, 1937-
    Monarchy / by Nathaniel Harris.
      p. cm. — (Systems of government)
    Includes bibliographical references and index.
    ISBN 0-8368-5885-9 (lib. bdg.)
    ISBN 0-8368-5890-5 (softcover)
    1. Monarchy—Juvenile literature. 2. Monarchy—History—Juvenile literature.
  I. Title. II. Series.
  JC375.H36   2005
  321'.6—dc22
                                                  2005042115

This North American edition first published in 2006 by
World Almanac® Library
A Member of the WRC Media Family of Companies
330 West Olive Street, Suite 100
Milwaukee, WI 53212 USA

This edition copyright © 2006 by World Almanac® Library. First published by Evans Brothers Limited.
Copyright © 2005 by Evans Brothers Limited, 2A Portman Mansions, Chiltern Street, London W1U 6NR,
United Kingdom. This U.S. edition published under license from Evans Brothers Limited.

Editor: Patience Coster
Designer: Jane Hawkins
Illustrations: Stefan Chabluk
Consultant: Michael Rawcliffe

World Almanac® Library editorial direction: Mark J. Sachner
World Almanac® Library art direction: Tammy West
World Almanac® Library production: Jessica Morris
World Almanac® Library editor: Gini Holland
World Almanac® Library designer: Kami Koenig

Photo credits: Archivo Iconografico S.A./Corbis 21, 23; The Bridgeman Art Library 6, 11, 14, 19;
The Bridgeman Art Library/Archives Charmet 10; The Bridgeman Art Library/Ashmolean Museum,
University of Oxford 15; The Bridgeman Art Library/City of Edinburgh Museums and Art Galleries,
Scotland 9; The Bridgeman Art Library/Egyptian National Museum, Cairo 13; The Bridgeman Art
Library/Leeds Museum and Art Galleries 22; Corbis 5; Gideon Mendel/Corbis 33; Giraudon/
The Bridgeman Art Library 12; Hulton-Deutsch Collection/Corbis 38; Mian Khursheed/Reuters/
Corbis 31; Reuters/Corbis 28; Susana/Vera/Reuters/Corbis 30; Tim Graham/Corbis 29, 36, 43;
Topham/ImageWorks 20; Topham Picturepoint 4, front cover and 24, 25, 34, 39, 42; Topham/
Polfoto 40; Topham/The British Library/HIP 8; Topham/UPPA 27, 41; Vittoriano Rastelli/Corbis 17.

Printed in the United States of America

1 2 3 4 5 6 7 8 9 09 08 07 06 05

CONTENTS

In this book, dates often appear in brackets after the names of individual monarchs. These are the monarch's reign dates, not birth or death dates. Dates are also written using B.C.E. and C.E. instead of B.C. and A.D., which are based on the Christian calendar. B.C.E. means "Before the Common Era" and replaces B.C. ("Before Christ"). C.E. means "in the Common Era" and replaces A.D. ("Anno Domini," which is Latin for "in the year of our Lord"). This book also uses the general term *state* when referring to all the varieties of independent political units (country, nation, federation, empire) and is not to be confused with the smaller units within some countries that are also called states, such as the fifty states making up the United States.

CHAPTER ONE

WHAT IS MONARCHY?

Queen Victoria, King Richard the Lionheart, King Arthur, the evil emperor in Star Wars—history and fiction have made kings, queens, emperors, and empresses famous. The individuals given these titles can be described as monarchs, a useful general word that covers them all. Monarchs have also been known by many other titles. Over the centuries, pharaohs, caesars, kaisers, czars, shahs, khans, and sultans have reigned in monarchies and made their mark on history.

Monarchy describes any form of government in which a monarch holds the highest office. In a monarchy, a titled individual such as a king is the sovereign (supreme ruler) and head of state and has normally inherited his or her position. Inherited power is what makes a monarchy different from the main alternative system of government in modern times—a republic.

In a republic, a president generally holds the highest office. In some countries, the president may have seized power by force, but in most instances he or she will have been elected. The present monarch of the United Kingdom (UK) is Queen Elizabeth II, who became queen in 1952 following the death of her father, King George VI. By contrast, in the United States, which is a republic, George W. Bush became president in 2001 after a nationwide

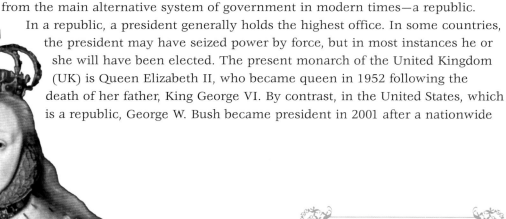

A portrait of royal authority: England's Queen Elizabeth I (1558–1603), holding the orb (right) and scepter.

GREEK ORIGINS

"Monarchy" comes from *monarchia,* a Greek word meaning "rule of one." The ancient Greeks were the first people to classify and analyze political systems.

▲ Royal pomp emphasizes the importance of monarchs. In this instance, Queen Elizabeth II and her husband Prince Philip are traveling in their gilded state coach to St. Paul's Cathedral, London, for a service to mark the Queen's Golden Jubilee (fiftieth anniversary) in June 2002. They also ride in it on important occasions such as the opening of Parliament.

election. Bush held office for four years and was elected to serve another four-year term (2005–2009). U. S. presidents may serve only two terms of office, unlike monarchs, who may rule for life.

ROYAL INHERITANCE

In most monarchies, the monarch reigns until he or she dies. Some monarchs, however, have chosen—or have been forced—to abdicate, which is to resign one's crown and allow a successor to take one's place. The crown is generally hereditary (inherited as if it were property) and passes from one member of the ruling family to the next. The

order of inheritance follows rules that reflect the origins of monarchy in a male-dominated world. Almost everywhere, the oldest son of the monarch inherits the throne, even if he has an older sister. If there are no sons, the oldest daughter inherits, which is why Queen Elizabeth II (the older of King George VI's two daughters) is the present sovereign of the UK.

If the monarch has no children, the nearest relation succeeds, with the same male-first principle continuing to be followed. The rules of inheritance have varied slightly from place to place. For example, when France was a monarchy (C.C.E. 500–1848), the Salic Law excluded females from inheriting the

KING-MAKING

Almost all monarchs go through some kind of ceremony at the beginning of their reigns. The most common ceremony is a coronation (literally "crowning"), which either creates or recognizes the monarch's royal authority. A Roman emperor was dressed in a purple cloak, and a laurel wreath was placed on his head. Then the acclamation followed—shouts that signified acceptance of the new monarch.

The Roman Emperor Constantine (C.E. 307–337) made the crown the chief symbol of his office. Then, in seventh-century Spain, the king was anointed with holy oil following the practice recorded in the Bible. Other insignia (symbols of authority) were introduced, notably the miter, scepter, and orb. Coronations became, and have remained, lavish, spectacular, and, for many people, deeply emotional events.

This painting from about 1620 shows how royal authority is handed down from one generation to the next. Akbar, the sixteenth-century Mogul Emperor of India, passes the crown from his son Jahangir to his grandson Shah Jahan. ▼

crown. Not surprisingly, most monarchs in history have been male. In spite of this, some of the most celebrated rulers have been women, from Hatshepsut (r. 1479–1458 B.C.E.) in Egypt to Queen Elizabeth I of England (r. C.E. 1558 –1603) and the Empress Catherine of Russia (r. C.E. 1762–1796).

Until very recent times, almost all states were monarchies. The exceptions were usually small countries, where it was possible for many citizens to take some part in government. In most places, slow communications and scattered populations meant that the permanent authority of one individual, a monarch, over a country was a more effective way to get things done. Monarchy also has the advantage of continuity: Power passes continuously from generation to generation. Ideally, when a monarch dies, the next in line takes over immediately, without any break in authority, as announced ceremonially by the French: "The king is dead: long live the king!"

ROYALTY AND NOBILITY

Most societies based on monarchy have been divided into ranks or classes with widely different powers and privileges. This arrangement is often shown as a pyramid-shaped diagram with the monarch at its top and the majority of people, or commoners, at its base. Between the two comes a number of privileged groups, of which the nobility, or aristocracy, is ranked directly below the monarch. Apart from the monarch's children (princes and princesses), nobles have titles such as duke, earl, baron, and lord, or their equivalents in other languages. At times, nobles have conspired or rebelled against monarchs. The highest noble families, however, are usually closely related to the royal family, and the monarch is the giver of titles and other honors. When the idea of monarchy is attacked, the nobility generally defends monarchy to protect its own status.

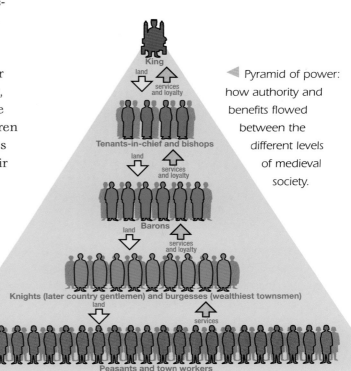

Pyramid of power: how authority and benefits flowed between the different levels of medieval society.

LORDS OF THE EARTH

For centuries, nomadic tribes moved over vast areas of northern Asia, grazing their flocks. Their superb horsemanship and sharp-shooting with arrows made them fearsome warriors. Whenever a gifted leader managed to unite the tribes, they posed a serious threat to the settled civilizations of Asia. The most successful of all was Temujin, creator of the Mongol Empire. Better known by the title of Genghis Khan ("Lord of the Earth"), Temujin was given this title in 1206, when he united the Mongol tribes and set out on a remarkable career of conquest. By the time of his death in 1227, Temujin's empire stretched from northern China to Persia and Eastern Europe. His sons were equally successful. His grandson, Kublai Khan (1259–94), became emperor of China. The Mongol Empire broke up soon afterward, but later Mogul conquerors (descendants of Mongols, Persians, and Turks) included Timur (1370–1405) and Babur (1526–1530).

▲ This fifteenth-century painting shows the coronation of a medieval king. The crown is placed on the king's head in the presence of four bishops. Most of those present are also members of the clergy. The religious aspect of coronations made kings sacred figures in the eyes of many subjects.

When they have been established for a long time, royal and noble families come to be thought of as special people. In Britain, they used to be described as "blue blooded," which implied that they were different from, and somehow better than, ordinary red-blooded people. The authority of a monarchy is greatly strengthened when the monarch is generally believed to be a special, superior being.

"Not all the water in the rough rude sea Can wash the balm from an anointed king, The breath of worldly men cannot depose The deputy elected by the Lord."

These lines come from *Richard II*, a play written by William Shakespeare in about 1595. Fearing that he may be deposed by his subjects, the king comforts himself with the belief that he has a divine right to rule because he is God's deputy on Earth.

DIVINE RULERS

In many cases, this idea has been very powerful because the monarch has been seen as a religious or divinely approved figure. Some monarchs have been believed to be gods or godlike. This was true, for example, of the pharaohs who ruled ancient Egypt. The emperors of Japan were also worshiped as divine until 1945; then, after Japan's defeat in World War II, the victors (the United States and its allies) made Emperor Hirohito admit to the Japanese people that he was not a god.

Most monarchs have not claimed to be divine, but many have relied heavily on the support of the state religion. Monarchs have often combined their state ceremonies with religious rituals and ceremonies, carried out with great pomp. For example, in Europe, a new monarch's right to rule was proclaimed by a coronation, held in a cathedral or abbey, and conducted by the Church in the presence of the highest nobility.

Tradition, inheritance, and religious ceremony worked together to make it appear to the people that monarchs had a right to rule. Many individuals developed an intense loyalty to their sovereigns and were prepared to fight and die in their defense. In 1642, the unpopular policies of King

Charles I of England led to a civil war between supporters of the king and supporters of Parliament (an assembly with an important role in making laws). When the war started, many who had disagreed with the king's actions rallied to his side, feeling that they could not fight against "His Sacred Majesty." Later, Charles's exiled descendants found devoted supporters, known as Jacobites (*see box, bottom right*), over several generations.

WIELDING POWER

Until recent centuries, monarchy aroused feelings of awe almost everywhere in the world, but the actual power wielded by monarchs has varied greatly. In some states, the monarch was a figure-head without any significant authority. In others, he or she was "the first among equals"—really just the leading noble in a society run by and for the nobility. In eighteenth-century Poland, the elect-ed king could do little without the consent of the nobility, even in an emergency. As a result, the country lacked decisive political leadership and, by 1795, had been divided between the powerful neighboring states of Prussia, Russia, and Austria.

"Divine" monarchs were not necessarily power-ful either. In some instances, their sacred status meant they were cut off from any kind of practi-cal activity. For centuries, the Japanese emperors were revered figures who lived quietly in their

Followers of Prince Charles Edward Stuart raise glasses to toast him. The prince failed to regain the throne for his father, but this painting shows the romantic appeal of his story and of the Jacobites' loyalty to his family. ▼

JACOBITE LOYALTY

In seventeenth-century England and Scotland, monarchs and Parliament were frequently in conflict. In 1688, King James II was driven into exile, and his son was barred from succeeding. The exiled king and his descen-dants made a number of attempts to recover the throne, relying on the loyalty to "the rightful king" still felt by many people. Their supporters, known as Jacobites (Jacobus is Latin for James), took part in several rebellions. In 1745, James's grandson, Prince Charles Edward ("Bonnie Prince Charlie"), led a Scottish Jacobite army deep into England before being forced back and defeated. The Jacobites failed, but their loyalty to their cause has always found admirers.

palaces while the country was actually ruled by a shogun, the leader of the dominant clan.

Most monarchs in history have wielded more power than these Japanese emperors. At the opposite extreme were rulers whose authority was almost unlimited. Their absolute power enabled them to kill or reward whomever they pleased and to sacrifice their subjects (the people they ruled) in great wars or huge construction ventures. Such monarchs are often described as autocrats or despots.

▲ A Chinese emperor holds court in an open-air pavilion, surrounded by nobles. Since he held "the Mandate of Heaven" (divine approval), the emperor was all powerful.

Famous autocrats include Shi Huang-ti (221–210 B.C.E.), the first Chinese emperor, who built the Great Wall of China, and Czar Peter I of Russia (1682–1725), who created the great city of St. Petersburg. Both achievements cost thousands of lives. Some autocrats have been moderate, well-meaning rulers, but access to such unchecked power has generally encouraged more vicious qualities. Several Roman emperors killed so many enemies, or people they believed to be their enemies, that no one felt safe. Such a reign usually ended suddenly when the emperor was assassinated or overthrown by his subjects.

A great many monarchies fell between these extremes of helplessness and despotism. The monarch had great power but was supposed to act according to the law. When vital decisions had to be made, he or she might be expected to consult some group of wise advisers, or nobles, or other representatives of the realm. In

THE IMPERIAL LINE

A series of monarchs belonging to the same family is known as a dynasty. Some dynasties have ruled for centuries. The longest lasting of all European dynasties was that of the Habsburgs.

From 1438 to 1806, the Habsburgs held the title of Holy Roman Emperor, which made them the recognized overlords of Germany and certain other parts of central Europe. They constantly added to their territories by making shrewd marriage alliances with other royal and noble families, and they reached the height of their power during the sixteenth and early seventeenth centuries. In the nineteenth century, the Habsburgs still ruled an Austrian empire covering much of southeast Europe. Catastrophic defeats during World War I (1914–1918) led to the breakup of the empire and the abdication of Charles I, ruler of Austria and Hungary, the last Habsburg emperor.

England, the king was advised from the thirteenth century onward by an assembly of great lords, leading churchmen, and representatives of the wealthier classes. By the seventeenth century, this assembly, known as Parliament, played such an important role in making laws and raising taxes that it came into conflict with the crown, or monarch, and eventually took over many royal powers.

Although the authority of monarchs and monarchies varied, monarchy as an institution remained essentially unchallenged until about 1770. Then, new political ideas and social changes began to have a tremendous impact. As a result, over the next two centuries many monarchies disappeared. Most of those that survived became constitutional monarchies—more or less democratic states, with elected governments, where the monarch had a limited but definite role to play.

In the twenty-first century, relatively few monarchies remain in the world. Those that remain, however, are surprisingly different from one another, reflecting their varied and colorful history.

MAGIC TOUCH

The sacred character of kingship remained strong until recent times. In England, as late as the eighteenth century, being touched by the monarch was believed to cure a tubercular disease called scrofula. For that reason, the disease was also known as "the king's evil."

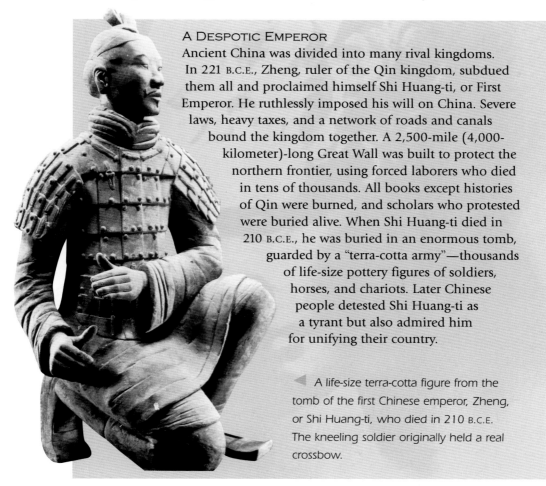

A DESPOTIC EMPEROR

Ancient China was divided into many rival kingdoms. In 221 B.C.E., Zheng, ruler of the Qin kingdom, subdued them all and proclaimed himself Shi Huang-ti, or First Emperor. He ruthlessly imposed his will on China. Severe laws, heavy taxes, and a network of roads and canals bound the kingdom together. A 2,500-mile (4,000-kilometer)-long Great Wall was built to protect the northern frontier, using forced laborers who died in tens of thousands. All books except histories of Qin were burned, and scholars who protested were buried alive. When Shi Huang-ti died in 210 B.C.E., he was buried in an enormous tomb, guarded by a "terra-cotta army"—thousands of life-size pottery figures of soldiers, horses, and chariots. Later Chinese people detested Shi Huang-ti as a tyrant but also admired him for unifying their country.

A life-size terra-cotta figure from the tomb of the first Chinese emperor, Zheng, or Shi Huang-ti, who died in 210 B.C.E. The kneeling soldier originally held a real crossbow.

CHAPTER TWO

EARLY MONARCHIES

Nobody knows exactly when the first monarchies were founded. Monarchy is generally believed to have appeared when early societies became complex, and specialized groups such as nobles, warriors, priests, and farmers developed. Such societies needed greater organization, so a single individual—a monarch—often came to control and direct them.

▲ The bronze head of a ruler from Akkad, an early state in Mesopotamia. Some believe it is a portrait of Sargon I, who ruled in about 2300 B.C.E.

THE FIRST CIVILIZATIONS

Monarchies already existed by the time the first civilizations appeared, in about 3000 B.C.E. Their centers were the lands of Sumer in Mesopotamia (present-day Iraq) and Egypt. Great rivers—the Tigris, the Euphrates, and the Nile—flowed through these regions, and the people of the area made large-scale efforts to control the rivers so that they fertilized the land and made it fruitful. The organization this required went along with some of the key features characteristic of a civilization: the growth of cities and the building of palaces and temples, and the development of governments, taxes, armies, and written records.

In about 1500 B.C.E., a new civilization developed independently in northern China, beginning a tradition that was to remain almost unbroken for 3,500 years. Gradually, ideas and skills from Mesopotamia, Egypt, and China spread to other lands, including India, Asia Minor (modern Turkey), Crete, and eastern Mediterranean states such as Canaan, Israel, Judah, and Phoenicia.

GOD-KINGS

In all these early civilizations, the king was regarded as a special, sacred person, utterly different from the rest of the people. He was the all-powerful ruler of the land and also its supreme religious figure. It was believed that he alone could make direct contact with the gods, ensuring that they would favor his people. The king was himself believed to be godlike. In fact, the kings of Egypt, known from about 1539 B.C.E. as pharaohs, were believed to be literally divine, because

One of many treasures found in the tomb of the boy pharaoh Tutankhamun, who died about 327 B.C.E. This bejeweled gold pectoral (chest ornament) displays a royal vulture.

each pharaoh was thought to be one of the greatest of the gods, Horus, in human form.

Sacred and all-powerful early kings gathered enormous wealth. Most of it has disappeared, but in the twentieth century archaeologists made some amazing discoveries. Beautifully crafted objects, rich in gold and other precious materials and dating from about 2600 B.C.E., were dug up among the remains of the Sumerian city of Ur in Iraq. The tomb of the pharaoh Tutankhamun contained even more spectacular finds. It was the only Egyptian royal tomb ever discovered with all its contents intact. Tutankhamun was about eighteen when he died (in about 1327 B.C.E.). He had not been very important, yet his tomb was filled with fabulous treasures.

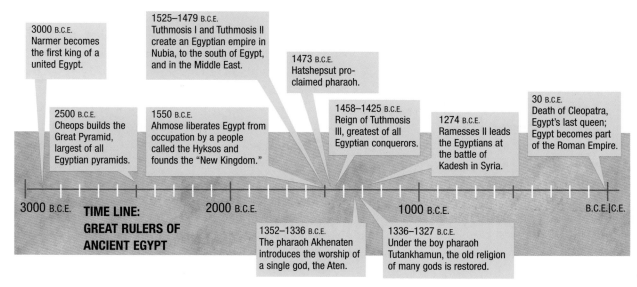

3000 B.C.E.
Narmer becomes the first king of a united Egypt.

1525–1479 B.C.E.
Tuthmosis I and Tuthmosis II create an Egyptian empire in Nubia, to the south of Egypt, and in the Middle East.

1473 B.C.E.
Hatshepsut proclaimed pharaoh.

30 B.C.E.
Death of Cleopatra, Egypt's last queen; Egypt becomes part of the Roman Empire.

2500 B.C.E.
Cheops builds the Great Pyramid, largest of all Egyptian pyramids.

1550 B.C.E.
Ahmose liberates Egypt from occupation by a people called the Hyksos and founds the "New Kingdom."

1458–1425 B.C.E.
Reign of Tuthmosis III, greatest of all Egyptian conquerors.

1274 B.C.E.
Ramesses II leads the Egyptians at the battle of Kadesh in Syria.

3000 B.C.E. **TIME LINE: GREAT RULERS OF ANCIENT EGYPT**

2000 B.C.E.

1000 B.C.E.

B.C.E.|C.E.

1352–1336 B.C.E.
The pharaoh Akhenaten introduces the worship of a single god, the Aten.

1336–1327 B.C.E.
Under the boy pharaoh Tutankhamun, the old religion of many gods is restored.

13

▲ A pharaoh's monuments to his own glory: The gigantic statue and the remains of a mighty temple are among many built by Ramesses II between 1279 and 1213 B.C.E.

LEADERS IN WAR

Royal wealth was increased by success in making war, which brought in plunder and slaves. In addition to their religious roles, kings were usually expected to lead armies in battle. Warfare became a much more organized affair with the development of civilizations. Armies grew as states expanded and clashed with one another—or with the nomadic (wandering) peoples who were attracted by their wealth. A king's personal standing depended on being victorious and, in the ancient world, monarchs are often portrayed trampling on their enemies. After one famous battle at Kadesh in Syria (1274 B.C.E.), both sides—Egyptians and Hittites—claimed to have triumphed. If, as seems likely, the result was actually a tie, the famous victory

monuments put up by the pharaoh Ramesses II are an early example of propaganda designed to impress the people.

Despite their supposedly sacred character, monarchs could lose their thrones and, as a result, their dynasties could disappear. Such changes could happen very quickly. The first Chinese emperor, Shi Huang-ti (see page 11), kept a firm grip on power until his death in 210 B.C.E. Then hatred of his harsh rule flared up. Soon his descendants had perished and a rebel leader founded the Han dynasty (202 B.C.E.–C.E. 220). Dynasties came and went, but the idea of an emperor ruling China as "the Son of Heaven" lasted 2,000 years, until 1911, when war and revolution ended monarchy in China.

The first European civilization grew up about 2200 B.C.E. on the island of Crete in the eastern Mediterranean. This picture shows a reconstruction of the palace's throne room at Knossos, based on archaeological finds. ▶

"If the ruler is upright [just], the people will imitate him as grass bends before the breeze."

The Chinese philosopher Confucius (c. 551–479 B.C.E.) on the role of a monarch.

EUROPE

The first European civilizations appeared about 2200 B.C.E. on the island of Crete and then, about 1600 B.C.E., in mainland Greece. Little is known of Cretan history, but the early Greeks (Mycenaeans) organized formidable, warrior-dominated kingdoms.

The great age of Greece, however, began much later (in the eighth century B.C.E.) and was based on city-states—relatively small states, each with a single city at its heart. Some of them were monarchies at first, but these were soon replaced. The Greeks invented a number of new political systems, including one in which all the citizens (but this meant males only and not slaves) took part in government. The Greeks called this arrangement "democracy." Athens became the most celebrated ancient democracy, leading Greek resistance to the greatest monarchy of its time, the Persian Empire.

HERO KINGS

The earliest Greeks, the Mycenaeans, flourished between about 1600 and 1150 B.C.E. Little is known of their deeds, but they appear in the *Iliad*, the first great literary work in Greek—and European—history. The *Iliad* is an epic poem by Homer. It was first written down in the eighth century B.C.E. but was composed earlier. It describes episodes in the war between the Greeks and the Trojans. The war famously ended when Greek warriors hid inside a gigantic wooden horse that the Trojans were fooled into taking inside their besieged city. The Greek warriors came out at night, opened the gates to their comrades, and the Trojans were massacred. Greek royal leaders such as Agamemnon of Mycenae and Nestor of Pylos are featured in many legends.

By the fourth century B.C., the Greek city-states' days of glory were over. They were dominated by Macedon, a neighboring state that had adopted Greek ways but remained a monarchy. Led by King Alexander of Macedon, who became known as Alexander the Great, the Macedonians and Greeks conquered the Persian Empire and most of the "known world" by 325 B.C.E.. Alexander's conquests spread the Greek language and culture over a huge area. He died in 323 B.C.E., when he was only thirty-three. His empire rapidly broke up into a handful of Greek kingdoms almost constantly at war with one another.

THE ROMAN EMPIRE

Meanwhile, Rome—a small city-state in Italy—was gradually becoming stronger. Rome began as a monarchy, but, in about 510 B.C.E., its king was driven out and a republic was set up. The event is known from legend rather than factual history, but hatred of the idea of a king became a strong Roman tradition.

Over the centuries, the Roman Republic conquered lands all round the Mediterranean Sea. Governing such a vast empire, however, was too much for the republic. Power passed to military leaders, and, after long and bloody civil wars, the most successful general, Julius Caesar, became ruler of the Roman world. Although Caesar refused the title "king," a group of conspirators, who believed that one-man rule would destroy the republic, assassinated him.

After further civil wars, Caesar's great-nephew, Augustus, emerged victorious in 30 B.C.E. He claimed to have restored the Roman Republic, and he made sure the old republican traditions were honored. In reality, however, Augustus had concentrated power in his own hands and ruled as he pleased. The kingly title was never revived, but Augustus and his successors became known as emperors.

> *"Monarchy is the one system of government where power is used for the good of all."*
>
> This statement was written by the Greek philosopher Aristotle in the fourth century B.C.E. and has often been quoted in praise of monarchy. Aristotle, however, was referring to benevolent monarchs who ruled for the benefit of their subjects. Aristotle contrasted monarchy with tyranny, the kind of monarchy in which the king rules for his own benefit. Clearly Aristotle recognized that there had been both good and bad monarchs.

HAIL, CAESAR!

Julius Caesar's great achievements led to his family name, Caesar, becoming one of the titles used by Roman emperors—even those who were not related to him. Down to the early twentieth century, the emperors of Germany and Russia were known as the kaiser and the czar, both versions of "Caesar." The words *emperor* and *imperial* come from the Latin word *imperator*, meaning "commander," a title used by the Roman emperor Augustus and his successors. Augustus avoided the title *king* because Romans hated the word. There has never been a clear-cut difference between a king and an emperor, but *emperor* tends to be used by the rulers of very large states, especially if there are many different peoples living as subjects in them.

The Roman emperors had a very mixed record of succesful rule. The bloodthirsty, reckless careers of Caligula (C.E. 37–41) and Nero (C.E. 54–68) have led some historians to believe they were insane. By contrast, "five good emperors" were said to have made the second century C.E. a Roman golden age of peace and prosperity. Later emperors were often successful generals who seized the throne, gaining or losing power while the empire was increasingly menaced by peoples outside it. In the fourth century, the empire became Christian, and one result was to strengthen the emperor's authority as a ruler chosen by God and blessed by the church. This important development carried over into Europe even when Roman power collapsed, and a new age began from the fifth century onward.

◄ These scenes of the all-conquering Roman army are among the many carved onto Trajan's Column in Rome, Italy, in C.E. 113. The carvings are the Romans' own record of the campaigns in Dacia (modern Romania) conducted by the Emperor Trajan (r. C.E. 98–117). The methodical way in which the soldiers are constructing fortifications—and their discipline as they prepare to board ship—display some of the qualities that made Rome great.

17

CHAPTER THREE

THE RISE AND DECLINE
OF MONARCHY

I n the fifth century, the western part of the Roman Empire broke up. Germanic tribes, often called Barbarians, took control from Britain to North Africa, setting up their own kingdoms. The eastern part of the Roman Empire survived. Once it separated from the Roman and Latin west, it became increasingly Greek in character, and it is generally known under the Greek name of Byzantium. Then, in the seventh century, most of Byzantium's Middle Eastern and North African territories were conquered by Arab invaders, inspired by the religion of Islam preached by the prophet Muhammad. By C.E. 711, the Islamic Empire stretched from Persia to southern Spain. Byzantium remained a force to be reckoned with; its territories included Anatolia (modern Turkey) and southeastern Europe.

Byzantium and the Islamic Empire (or Caliphate) were ruled by monarchs who wielded supreme political and religious authority. One of the Byzantine emperors' titles was "Autocrator" (the word *autocrat* comes from Greek), while the caliph, or Islamic ruler, was called the "Commander of the Faithful," because he was also a religious leader.

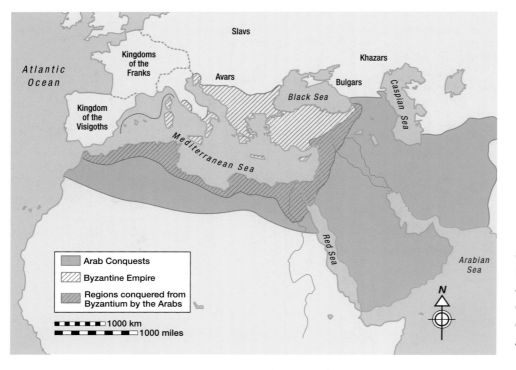

◀ This map shows the Byzantine Empire and the extent of Islamic Arab conquests by about C.E. 700.

New peoples gained power in Europe about C.E. 500. This manuscript illustration shows an episode in the lives of Clovis, king of the Franks, and Alaric, king of the Visigoths.

"BARBARIAN" EUROPE

The Germanic kings of Europe had nothing like this authority, and their war-torn realms were backward in comparison with the Byzantine and Islamic empires. The Germanic kings were at first little more than tribal war leaders, elected by their companions in arms. The kings were usually chosen from a single family, but there was no automatic succession by inheritance. In particular, a child had little chance of succeeding in the rough, post-Roman world, or, if he did, he rarely survived for long. In the Germanic kingdoms, the church generally supported the monarchy, devising ceremonies that emphasized its sacred character. Even so, among Germanic peoples such as the Franks and the Visigoths, kingship was a dangerous occupation, and their history is filled with treacheries, assassinations, and massacres.

After centuries of wars, migrations, and invasions by outside peoples, Europe began to settle down, and distinct national groups such as the

French and Germans evolved. About C.E. 1000, Europe entered the period known as the Middle Ages, which lasted until about 1500. The hereditary nature of kingship became more firmly established, but royal powers were still limited by lack of material resources, poor communications, and their political and social systems. Medieval monarchs sometimes behaved badly, but law and custom generally restricted their actions. The nobility, the church, towns, and other bodies had "liberties" (privileges) and rights that monarchs could not interfere with. In many states, monarchs found it wise to listen to the opinions of councils of leading men or assemblies of people representing various classes (for example, the English Parliament and similar bodies in France and Scotland).

In time, nations such as England, France, and Scotland became united under their own kings. In contrast, in Germany and Italy there were many states, widely different in size and influence. The Holy Roman Emperor (*see box, below*) was the overlord of Germany and other parts of central Europe, but despite his grand title, he had little control over individual states such as Saxony, Brandenburg, and Bavaria, which became more, not less, independent over time. In Italy, the rival states included the central Italian territories ruled by the pope, the head of the Catholic Church.

"NEW" MONARCHIES

In the late Middle Ages, the monarchies of Western Europe gradually became more powerful. By the sixteenth century, this tendency was so marked that many historians describe states such as England, France, and Spain as "New Monarchies."

Their "newness" lay in their increasing riches and ability to control their subjects. Royal government was now efficiently conducted by well-trained bureaucracies—sets of officials who ran the state and collected taxes. "Liberties" were removed and royal law was imposed across the realm. The great nobles submitted to royal authority and served it, or were humbled. The church, too, lost much of its nonspiritual power. A royal army made sure that royal policy was enforced. This army was generally stronger

▲ Trained civil servants extended the power of the "New Monarchies" of sixteenth-century Europe. Here, an English tax collector is making sure that the state receives its due.

than any opposing local force of noble retainers or rebellious commoners.

The growth in royal authority took place over a long period and often experienced setbacks. Many developments, however, favored a strengthening of state power, including eco-

---

MIGHTY WEAK

The Holy Roman Empire extended over Germany and some other parts of central Europe. In the Middle Ages, the emperor was regarded by most people as the leader of Christendom. His real power, in fact, was very limited, largely because each emperor had to be elected by other German rulers. These electors wanted to be as independent as possible and were able to bargain advantageously with candidates for the imperial title. As a result, Holy Roman Emperors had few resources and were only effective if they had lands, wealth, and followers of their own. There were some famous medieval emperors, such as Frederick I Barbarossa (1155–1190) and Frederick II (1220–1250), and later the Habsburg dynasty made the imperial title practically hereditary. Yet none of them managed to turn the Holy Roman Empire into a single state such as England or France. By 1806, the imperial title had become so meaningless that the Emperor Francis II resigned it, and the Holy Roman Empire ceased to exist.

nomic expansion, the increasing cost of waging war, and the sixteenth-century Reformation, a movement which divided Christians into Catholics and Protestants and thus weakened the church's resistance to state control.

During the same period, Europeans developed oceangoing ships and began to explore the New World and trade directly with Africa and Asia. As a result, Europeans came in contact with a variety of other monarchies, including Mexico's Aztec emperors, the Incas of Peru, and African kings such as those of Mbanza Kongo and Dahomey.

▲ This picture shows Montezuma, emperor of the Aztecs in Central America. The arrival of the Spanish in 1520 led to his death and the destruction of Aztec civilization.

ABSOLUTISM

The strengthening of the state continued into the seventeenth century, and monarchs benefited in status as well as power. This was the age of absolutism (unrestrained royal rule), the most celebrated example being King Louis XIV of France, who was the dominant figure in Europe for most of his long reign (1643–1715).

Louis was served by able ministers, but he—not they—made the vital decisions. The king's personal power was so great that a letter sent by him was enough to have a man put in prison

AMERICAN EMPERORS

The Americas have been inhabited for at least 20,000 years, and advanced societies appeared there by 1150 B.C.E. When Europeans arrived in the early sixteenth century, there were two great American civilizations which had recently been united into empires—by the Aztecs in Central America, and by the Incas in Peru and neighboring territories in South America. Although they were far apart, the positions of their monarchs were similar. The Aztec and Incan emperors were such sacred figures that their subjects were forbidden to look them in the face. In the 1520s and 1530s, small groups of Spanish adventurers were able to overthrow both empires. One reason for their success was that in each case they seized the emperor and ruled through him. The people only began to resist when it was too late. The Aztecs' and Incas' independence was lost, and their religion and whole way of life were destroyed.

A scene from the English Civil War, 1645: the parliamentary leader, Oliver Cromwell, storms a royalist stronghold.

MONARCHS AND REPUBLICS

England was an exception to the absolutist trend. Kings and queens of the Tudor dynasty, such as Henry VIII (1509–1547) and Elizabeth I (1558–1603), strengthened the state but worked with parliament. This meant that laws

for an indefinite period. On the other hand, the European tradition of respect for law and custom was very strong, and in practice this tradition helped put limits on royal power. In most cases, absolutism, despite its literal meaning, was not the same as autocracy. Most European kings knew that they had to respect the law if they were to maintain their dynasties.

continued to be passed and taxes raised jointly by the monarch (also known as "the crown") and Parliament. So, when political and religious conflicts developed, Parliament was strong enough to challenge the crown. In fact, parliamentary forces won a civil war in 1642–1649 against King Charles I. He was beheaded, and for a few years England was a republic. In 1660,

NAMES AND NUMBERS

The supporters of a monarchy believe in its right to rule. If it falls, they behave as though the new sovereign or government does not exist. As far as they are concerned, the fallen monarch continues to rule, followed by his, or her, descendants. This explains some curious numberings of monarchs.

Louis XVI was deposed during the French Revolution and executed in 1793. Eventually, in 1814, the monarchy was restored and his brother became king—as Louis XVIII. As far as royalists were concerned, Louis XVI's young son had reigned as Louis XVII, although he was held prisoner until he died, within a year or two of his father, at about the age of ten. Similarly, the Emperor Napoleon I was succeeded by his nephew, who called himself Napoleon III (1852–1870), in spite of the fact that Napoleon I's son had also never ruled.

"All kings is mostly rapscallions [rascals]."

A scornful republican view from *The Adventures of Huckleberry Finn* (1884) by the American writer Mark Twain.

King Charles II was restored to the throne, but, in 1688, another political-religious crisis led to the exile of his brother, King James II. This, the "Glorious Revolution" of 1688, was made strong by new laws passed by Parliament. These laws created a political system in which both crown and Parliament had important roles, with policies formed by ministers who needed the support of both institutions. Known as a constitutional monarchy, this type of monarchy strictly defines the crown's legal powers.

In 1707, England and Scotland were united to create the kingdom of Great Britain. The term "Britain" has continued in common use, although from 1801, when Ireland became part of the state, the correct name became the United Kingdom. As a result of later political changes, the full name became the present "United Kingdom of Great Britain and Northern Ireland," commonly abbreviated to "the UK." Britain steadily grew stronger through the eighteenth and nineteenth centuries, pioneering the Industrial Revolution and acquiring an enormous overseas empire through trade and conquest. During the same period, the powers of the monarch were gradually transferred to the elected government. Under Queen Victoria (1837–1901), Britain's modern constitutional monarchy took shape.

In North America, thirteen of Britain's colonies rebelled, and, in 1783, they won the Revolutionary War and formed the United States of America (U.S.). This new republic represented the first important challenge to monarchy in modern times. Soon afterward, a revolution in France led to the founding of a republic there. The French Republic was short-lived, although its basically democratic ideals continued to have a strong influence. The republic was replaced by a new French monarchy, the Empire. In a brief but spectacular career, General Napoleon Bonaparte

◀ Napoleon Bonaparte early in his career of conquest, leading his troops across the Alps into Italy in 1800.

THE CZARS

The Russian monarchy was founded by Scandinavian warriors who built Kiev, now the capital of the Ukraine. The first prince of Kiev was Oleg (893–924). Later on, Russia broke up into many rival states. It was gradually reunited by the grand dukes of Moscow. Ivan IV (1533–1584), often called Ivan the Terrible, proclaimed himself czar, or emperor, and all his successors used the title. In 1613, Michael Romanov founded the imperial dynasty which ruled until 1917. Russia was vast but undeveloped, although Peter the Great (1682–1725) gained territory on the Baltic Sea, bringing the country into contact with more developed European societies. All the czars were autocrats, often violent and unpredictable. The last czar, Nicholas II, was forced to abdicate after a revolution in February 1917. A year later, he and his family were shot.

made himself Emperor of the French (1805–1814, 1815) and put members of his family on several European thrones. With the defeat of Napoleon in 1815, however, the old dynasties he had replaced were restored. France had a turbulent nineteenth-century history, finally opting in 1870 for a republic.

Most parts of Central and South America also became republics. Elsewhere, monarchy remained the norm. In Europe, Germany was united as an empire ruled by a kaiser, and the different Italian states were fused into a single kingdom. The Holy Roman Empire dissolved, but the Habsburgs built up a large but ramshackle Austrian Empire in southeast Europe, which included what are now the countries of Austria, the Czech Republic, Slovakia, Hungary, Slovenia, Croatia, and Bosnia.

APPROACHING CRISIS

Before the end of the nineteenth century, some form of constitutional monarchy had been established in most European countries. Russia under the czars and Ottoman Turkey under its sultans, however, were still autocracies. Russia ruled over most of northern and central Asia, and the Turkish Empire covered much of the Middle East and the Balkans. In the rest of Asia and Africa, vast territories had become colonies of Britain, Portugal, and other European countries, although local kings and chiefs were sometimes left in place under the "protection" of the colonial power. Some coun-

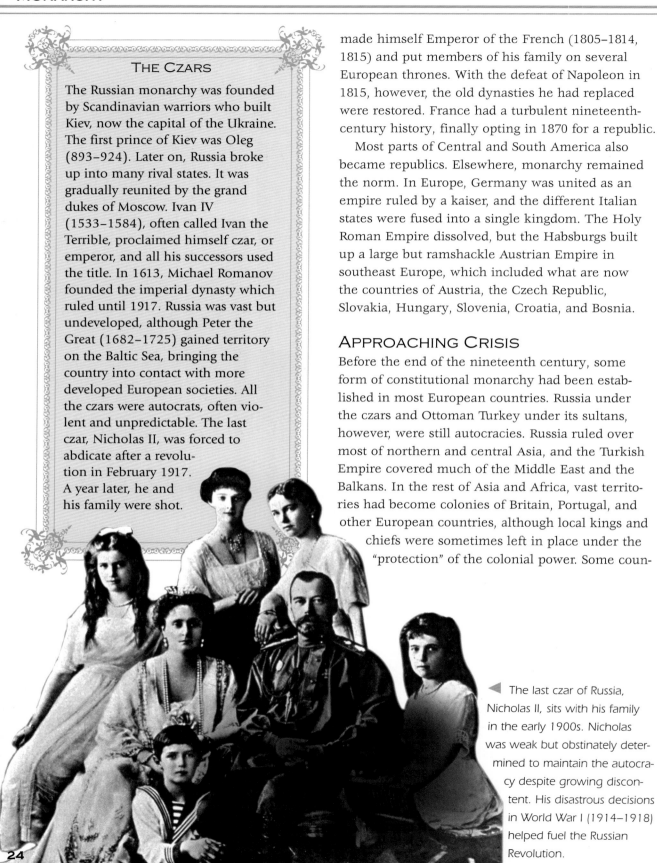

The last czar of Russia, Nicholas II, sits with his family in the early 1900s. Nicholas was weak but obstinately determined to maintain the autocracy despite growing discontent. His disastrous decisions in World War I (1914–1918) helped fuel the Russian Revolution.

Monarchs in exile: Manuel II of Portugal (top left behind his mother) with Spain's Alfonso XIII (grandfather of the present Spanish king) leave London's Ritz hotel in the 1930s. ▶

TIME LINE: THE FALL OF EUROPEAN MONARCHIES IN THE TWENTIETH CENTURY

1918
Germany: November 9, Kaiser Wilhelm II abdicates and flees as revolution breaks out and Germany slides to defeat in World War I. The kings of Bavaria, Württemberg, and Saxony also lose their thrones.

Austria-Hungary: November 11, the defeated empire is disintegrating and Charles I abdicates.

1931
Spain: King Alfonso XIII is overthrown and a republic declared. (His son, Juan Carlos I, is restored in 1975.)

1946
Italy: The monarchy is discredited by its role in World War II. In June, King Umberto II leaves after Italians vote for a republic.

Bulgaria: In September, King Simeon II is exiled after a communist takeover.

1973
Greece: King Constantine (in exile since 1967) abdicates when Greeks vote against the return of the monarchy.

1900   1925   1950   1975

1910
Portugal: King Manuel II flees following a national revolt.

1917
Russia: Czar Nicholas is forced to abdicate after the Russian Revolution; he and his family are shot in 1918.

1939
Albania: King Zog I flees as the country is invaded by Italy.

1945
Yugoslavia: King Peter II, in exile since 1941, is deposed as communists take power.

1947
Romania: Communists overthrow King Michael I.

---

tries did manage to keep their independence, notably the Chinese and Japanese empires and the kingdom of Thailand.

Still apparently dominant in 1900, monarchy was almost destroyed by the upheavals of the twentieth century. In 1911, a revolution overthrew the 2,000-year-old Chinese Empire. World War I (1914–1918) led to the collapse of the German, Austro-Hungarian, Russian, and Turkish empires. After World War II (1939–1945), the monarchs of Italy and Eastern Europe lost their thrones. In the 1940s and 1950s, changes

in the Arab world replaced most of its monarchies with republics. As the former colonies of the European empires became independent between 1945 and 1975, most of them chose to become republics. As late as 1973, a European monarchy, Greece, was abolished.

The remaining monarchies include some powerful and important states. They continue to be remarkably varied, reflecting both the traditions of their cultures and, often, the impact of modern and global influences on traditions that were born in ancient, isolated times.

CHAPTER FOUR

MODERN MONARCHIES

T oday there are relatively few monarchies, but they are still found all over the globe. In Europe there are seven kingdoms, all of them constitutional monarchies.

EUROPEAN MONARCHIES

The UK consists of England, Wales, Scotland, and Northern Ireland, countries brought together over the centuries by conquest or dynastic marriages. The present sovereign is Queen Elizabeth II (born 1926). The long history of the monarchy and the way in which it has adapted to democratic institutions are reflected in elaborate ceremonies and in political forms and traditions that have been left over from the past.

As a result, British monarchs still appear to be very powerful. In theory, the monarch can declare war and appoint ministers and has many other government powers (known as the royal prerogative). The monarch is also part of the lawmaking process. Laws are made by "the Queen in Parliament," and all need the queen's assent (agreement).

The reality of the situation is very different. A British monarch does not make any important political decision. She or he always acts on "advice," usually that given by the current prime minister. Therefore, it is the prime minister or the government that actually makes the decisions and makes use of the prerogative and other royal powers. This is one reason why the term "the crown" is so often used: It avoids any suggestion that the queen is personally involved, for example, in a legal case brought by "the crown" (the state prosecutors). Because the government makes all political decisions, the Queen cannot be blamed for them. She is regarded as being "above politics." Taking no sides, she can therefore be seen as deserving the loyalty of the entire people.

As a rule, all political responsibility falls on the elected government. Prime ministers, however, can

NOT BRITISH

Two places in the British Isles, the Isle of Man and the Channel Islands, are not part of the UK, although they owe allegiance to the crown. English monarchs once also held the separate title of dukes of Normandy, a region in France. Then, in 1205, the French king conquered all of mainland Normandy. The Channel Islands were all that was left of the duchy, and therefore they belong to the crown but are not part of Britain. The Isle of Man and the Channel Islands have their own assemblies (equivalent to Britain's parliament) and run their own affairs, but the British government takes charge of their defense and foreign relations.

▲ Britain's Queen Elizabeth II makes the Speech from the Throne in 2003; her husband, Prince Philip, is seated beside her.

sometimes benefit from the advice of an experienced monarch, and it is just possible that, in some unusual situation, the monarch might have to intervene. This occurred during a political and economic crisis in 1930, when King George V persuaded the prime minister, Ramsey Macdonald, to stay in office and try to form a new "national" government. Macdonald did so, with important consequences, including a split in his own Labour Party, which changed the entire balance of political forces.

The once enormous British Empire dissolved in the late twentieth century, as peoples in Britain's colonies won their independence. Now only a handful of overseas territories, such as Gibraltar and the Falkland Islands, are still under British rule. Many former British colonies belong to the Commonwealth, a friendly association of fully independent countries. The British monarch is the head of the Commonwealth, but this is a purely hon-

ROYAL DUTIES

Most of a constitutional monarch's actions are symbolic or ceremonial, which means they do not affect politics. Britain's Queen Elizabeth II opens Parliament at the beginning of every annual session. She then reads the "Speech from the Throne"—a speech that is written for her by the government — and outlines its future policies. She has to sign Acts of Parliament (the royal assent) before they become law. She confers knighthoods and other honors (acting on government advice). She also meets foreign ambassadors, makes good will visits as head of state to other countries, and keeps in touch with her subjects by being present at all sorts of occasions such as the opening of a new hospital or the staging of a popular sporting event. The Queen's political duties involve reading state documents and a weekly meeting with the prime minister.

orary position, with no actual power. There are also fifteen ex-imperial countries, formerly ruled by the United Kingdom, that are now independent but have chosen to retain the Queen as head of state—that is, holding the same position as she holds in Britain. She therefore reigns as a constitutional monarch in each of these sixteen countries (including the UK), which are quite separate from one another. Since she cannot be in more than one place at a time, she resides in Britain and is represented in each of the other countries by a governor-general, who carries out all the royal duties. The governor-general is appointed by the Queen on the advice of the government of the country in question. Queen Elizabeth is currently the sovereign of Canada, Australia, and New Zealand. She also rules many

> *"To advise, to encourage, and to warn."*
>
> These were the political duties of the British monarch according to Walter Bagehot's influential book *The English Constitution,* published in 1867.

states in or close to the Caribbean, namely Belize and the island nations of Jamaica, Antigua, and Barbuda, the Bahamas, Barbados, Grenada, St. Kitts and Nevis, St. Lucia, and St. Vincent and the Grenadines;and she is the sovereign of three other island states, Papua New Guinea, the Solomons, and Tuvalu. All of these separate countries have democratic parliamentary systems similar to Britain's, and the crown has a similar role in each.

CONTINENTAL KINGDOMS

Six European kingdoms are run on broadly similar lines to the UK, however different the ceremonial procedures may be (Norway, for example, has no coronation). In other words, royal prestige is great, but the elected government exercises any powers that the monarch may have as head of state.

Jamaican children greet Britain's Queen Elizabeth II with enthusiasm as she passes through the island's capital, Kingston, in 2002. The trip was part of the celebrations marking her fiftieth anniversary as queen. ▼

▲ England, June 2002: a gathering of the reigning sovereigns of Europe and their husbands and wives. They are celebrating the Golden Jubilee of Queen Elizabeth II (center), who came to the throne in 1952.

Denmark has been a monarchy since the tenth century. One of its kings, Cnut (Canute), also ruled England and Norway. Females have been allowed to inherit Denmark's throne since 1952, which made it possible for the present monarch, Margrethe, to become queen in 1972. Norway was an independent kingdom during the early Middle Ages, but from the fourteenth century it was dominated by Denmark or Sweden. In 1905, Norway broke away from Sweden, electing a Danish prince as its king.

The Swedish kingdom is also ancient, although it was overshadowed by Denmark until the seventeenth century, when Sweden was briefly a major military power controlling wide territories around the Baltic Sea. Present-day Sweden is strongly democratic and committed to equality. The constitution firmly states that the monarch is head of state but takes

DOTS ON THE MAP

Four tiny European monarchies that can get overlooked easily on a map are the principalities of Andorra, Liechtenstein, Monaco, and the Grand Duchy of Luxembourg. All are constitutional monarchies, but because of their small size, the wealth and prestige of the ruling family tends to have considerable influence. In Liechtenstein, where the importance of the financial industry creates special circumstances, voters agreed in 2003 to increase the prince's powers after he threatened to move out of the country. The strangest arrangement is found in Andorra, which is ruled by "co-princes:" currently the president of France and the bishop of Urgel in northern Spain!

no part in government. The eldest child, whether male or female, inherits the throne.

An independent Netherlands was created in 1598, when the provinces of what are now the Netherlands and Belgium revolted against Spanish rule. Only the seven northern provinces were successful, becoming the Dutch Republic

▲ In April 2004, King Juan Carlos speaks to the Spanish Parliament in Madrid at its opening session. Unlike British royalty, he wears no crown when addressing parliament.

or the Netherlands. For centuries, the Orange family occupied the highest political and military office in the republic; its members included William of Orange who became king of England (r. 1689–1702) in partnership with his wife Mary. In 1815, a member of the Orange family, William I (r. 1815–1840) became the first king of the Netherlands. The Netherlands is another monarchy where succession to the throne is in order of birth, regardless of gender.

After the 1598 revolt, Spain reconquered the provinces to the south of the Netherlands. They were ruled in turn by Spain, Austria, and the Netherlands until 1830, when they broke away from the Netherlands, took the name Belgium, and invited a German prince (Leopold, uncle of Britain's Queen Victoria) to become king.

Spain became a united and powerful kingdom in the late fifteenth century and spearheaded the European discovery and conquest of the Americas. Spain's sixteenth-century "Golden Age" was followed by a long decline. In the nineteenth century, the monarchy became involved in the civil wars fought between rival political groups. Further conflicts devastated twentieth-century Spain until a constitutional monarchy was established under King Juan Carlos I (r. 1975–).

ROYAL DEMOCRAT

Spain's turbulent history has caused King Juan Carlos I to play a much more active political role than most European monarchs. Spain became a republic in 1931, but after the ferocious Spanish Civil War (1936–1939), the victor, General Francisco Franco, established a military dictatorship. Franco did not restore the monarchy during his lifetime, but he arranged that Juan Carlos should become king after his death, which took place in 1975. Franco believed that Juan Carlos would maintain the general's anti-democratic brand of conservatism. Juan Carlos, instead, chose advisers who helped him to move cautiously toward a democratic Spain, established in the constitution of 1978. Later, in 1981, a lieutenant-colonel in the Civil Guard held the entire Spanish parliament as hostages, intending to start an anti-democratic revolution. The king's firm opposition to the plot was an important factor in its rapid collapse. Since then, Spain has functioned as a stable constitutional monarchy.

HOLY MONARCH

The Vatican City-State is almost impossible to classify. It is the world's smallest state, effectively a palace in the middle of the Italian capital, Rome. The pope, the head of the worldwide Roman Catholic Church, lives in the Vatican. As the absolute sovereign of the city-state and its approximately 900 inhabitants, he can be described as a monarch. The papal monarchy is unusual, because popes are elected (by an assembly of cardinals), and there is no hereditary aspect to this essentially spiritual office.

THE MIDDLE EAST

Most of the Middle East was ruled between the fourteenth and nineteenth centuries by the sultans of the Ottoman Turkish Empire. Separate kingdoms developed in the region as the Turkish Empire weakened, and others were set up after it fell in 1922. Many of these monarchies were replaced by republics in the late twentieth century, but some have so far survived the political upheavals of the region.

The largest Middle Eastern monarchy is Saudi Arabia, a mainly desert kingdom which extends over most of the Arabian peninsula. It was created by Ibn Saud, who conquered a number of previously separate territories between 1913 and 1925. In 1932, the royal family's name, Saud, became part of the kingdom's title. Since then, Saudi Arabia has become wealthy, thanks to its vast reserves of oil. This wealth may have made it easier for the Saud family to maintain an absolute monarchy. The king chooses and heads the government, and members of the royal family occupy the other leading positions. Politics in Saudi Arabia are complicated by the fact that it is a holy land to Muslims (followers of Islam). There is some

◄ The Saudi Crown Prince (heir to the throne), Abdullah bin Abdul Aziz, on a visit to Pakistan in October 2003. He inspects an honor guard of Pakistani soldiers in the capital, Islamabad.

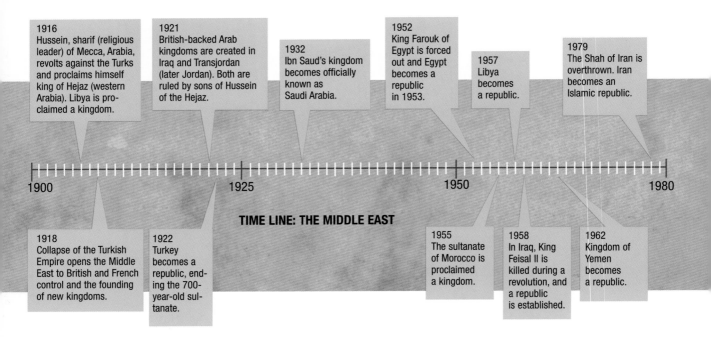

1916
Hussein, sharif (religious leader) of Mecca, Arabia, revolts against the Turks and proclaims himself king of Hejaz (western Arabia). Libya is proclaimed a kingdom.

1921
British-backed Arab kingdoms are created in Iraq and Transjordan (later Jordan). Both are ruled by sons of Hussein of the Hejaz.

1932
Ibn Saud's kingdom becomes officially known as Saudi Arabia.

1952
King Farouk of Egypt is forced out and Egypt becomes a republic in 1953.

1957
Libya becomes a republic.

1979
The Shah of Iran is overthrown. Iran becomes an Islamic republic.

1900   1925   1950   1980

TIME LINE: THE MIDDLE EAST

1918
Collapse of the Turkish Empire opens the Middle East to British and French control and the founding of new kingdoms.

1922
Turkey becomes a republic, ending the 700-year-old sultanate.

1955
The sultanate of Morocco is proclaimed a kingdom.

1958
In Iraq, King Feisal II is killed during a revolution, and a republic is established.

1962
Kingdom of Yemen becomes a republic.

opposition to Saudi absolutism in the country, and Middle Eastern wars and terrorism are also severe threats to its stability.

The ruling family of neighboring Jordan, the Hashemites, is descended from an Arabian leader driven out by Ibn Saud. The British installed Hashemite dynasties in Iraq and Jordan following the Turkish collapse in 1922. The Iraqi monarchy was overthrown in 1958, but King Hussein of Jordan (r. 1953–1999) managed to survive a period when traditional monarchies were under pressure to modernize. Dependent during this time on loyal desert warriors and his own shrewdness, Hussein later moved toward a constitutional monarchy. This was effectively established by 1991, when political parties were legalized.

The other Middle Eastern monarchies consist of small but oil-rich states in or close to the Arabian peninsula and the Persian Gulf. They are Bahrain, Kuwait, Qatar, the United Arab Emirates, and Oman. Most of these have been ruled for centuries by sultans or emirs whose authority is absolute, although in 2001, Bahrain

became a constitutional monarchy. Some changes have taken place in Kuwait since it was invaded by Iraq in 1990. The invasion ended when a United Nations force intervened, and the limited democratic element was strengthened in Kuwait. Neither Kuwaiti women nor the huge numbers of foreign workers in the country, however, can vote. The crown prince heads the government.

AFRICA

The nations of North Africa are mainly Muslim and are more closely linked to the Middle East than to the rest of Africa. The only remaining kingdom in North Africa is Morocco. The Alawite dynasty has reigned there since the seventeenth century, although under French and Spanish control between 1912 and 1956. Morocco is a constitutional monarchy, but the king's position of religious authority as "Commander of the Faithful" has helped him to retain considerable power. Monarchy has a long history in Africa, notably in Benin (formerly Dahomey) and in the former Kongo Kingdom of Central Africa, which had

▲ *Royal ceremonial in Swaziland, June 2004: King Mswati III has just returned from a state visit to Kenya. While he stands at attention during the playing of the national anthem, traditionally dressed security guards watch out for trouble. Crowned on April 25, 1986, at the age of eighteen, King Mswati III succeeded his father, King Sobhuza II, who liberated his country from the British and ruled from 1921 to 1982.*

diplomatic relations with Portugal from the fifteenth century; among the Zulus of South Africa; and in Ethiopia. Only the Ethiopian monarchy survived into the twentieth century. The Emperor Haile Selassie claimed descent from the Biblical King Solomon and is still regarded as a spiritual leader by the Rastafarian religious group. He ruled Ethiopia from 1930 to 1936, when Italian forces occupied the country. He returned from exile in 1941 and reigned until he was deposed by an army mutiny in 1974.

There are now only two monarchies in the whole of Africa south of the Sahara. Independent since 1966, Lesotho is entirely enclosed by South African territory. Its politics have been complicated by army interference, but since 1993 it has been a constitutional monarchy. In Swaziland in southern Africa, the king has great power, although a mainly elected assembly exists. Political parties are not allowed, and the influence of tradition is strong.

THE LAST EMPEROR

Only a few new monarchies have been created in the last century. The most recent was in the Central African Republic. An impoverished country with about two million citizens, the republic became independent of France in 1960. At the end of 1965, an army officer, Colonel Jean Bedel Bokassa, seized power and made himself president. In 1977, he had himself crowned Emperor Bokassa I in a lavish ceremony modeled on the coronation of Napoleon I of France in 1804. The country became the Central African Empire—but only until 1979, when Bokassa was overthrown. He seems likely to have been the world's last new emperor.

ASIA

As in the Middle East, monarchies in Asia have not found it easy to deal with conflicts between tradition and the demands of the modern world. The most successful has been Japan, for the surprising reason that it was defeated in World War II (1939–1945) and then occupied. The emperor, previously worshipped as a divine being, was forced by the United States and its allies to admit publicly that he was not divine. The 1947 constitution recognized him as the symbol of the nation but denied him any political role. Since then, Japan has functioned as a prosperous parliamentary democracy.

Four of Asia's seven monarchies are situated in Southeast Asia. In Thailand, the monarchy has existed since 1782 and was absolute until 1932.

It has remained widely revered by ordinary Thais but has played an unclear role in politics. Parliamentary systems have been established and scrapped many times, not by the king but by the army. In the early 2000s, there were hopeful signs that Thailand was beginning to develop into a working constitutional monarchy, although, as yet, political parties have not been allowed.

Neighboring Cambodia has an extraordinary history. It became independent of France in 1953, but its king, Norodom Sihanouk, disliked his lack of power as a constitutional monarch. He abdicated and began a career as a politician. In the 1970s and 1980s, a long period of bloodshed and chaos followed, at its worst in 1975–1978, when the communist Khmer Rouge were responsible for mass killings. Subsequently, the Cambodians were so

The royal line continues: In 2002, King Bhumibol and Queen Sirikit of Thailand take part in the ceremony in which their grandchild is named. ▼

bitterly divided that the United Nations took over the country and set up a new, democratic political system. It began to function in 1993 with a now aged Norodom Sihanouk reoccupying the throne—a royal recovery that is unprecedented in modern times.

Malaysia, to the south of Thailand, is a federation. A federation consists of a number of states or provinces that have united while continuing to control many of their own affairs. Federations can be headed by a constitutional monarch, a president, or another central authority. The United States, Canada, and Australia are examples of federations. The Malaysian states have an unusual system for electing their supreme head. The rulers of the seven mainland states elect one of their number to the position to serve a five-year term. Most decisions are made by the elected government, so this ruler is a constitutional monarch.

The remaining three Asian monarchies are very small. In Brunei, on the island of Borneo, the sultan wields absolute power. As in the Gulf States, this is more easily tolerated because the possession of oil reserves has given Brunei a very high standard of living. In two relatively remote Himalayan kingdoms, Nepal and Bhutan, royal and religious traditions remain strong, although from the 1990s moves were made in both countries to give the people a greater say.

In the Pacific area, the island group of Samoa is a constitutional monarchy. Its king is head of state for life, but future heads of state will be elected for five-year terms. In Tonga, the tradition-based authority of the king is very great. In the assembly, elected members are a minority, and the current prime minister is one of the king's sons.

ASIAN DYNASTIES

- China had a long history of kingdoms and dynasties even before Shi Huang-ti united the country in 221 B.C.E. Famous imperial dynasties included the Han (202 B.C.E.–C.E. 220), the Tang (618–907), the Song (960–1279), the Ming (1368–1644) and the Qing, or Manchus (1644–1912). China became a republic in 1911.

- Japan's first emperor was the legendary Jimmu (r. c. 660–585 B.C.E.). All subsequent Japanese emperors claimed to be descended from him. The present emperor is Akihito (r. 1989–   ).

- The subcontinent of India has been ruled by many dynasties, although few have controlled the entire region. The Moguls invaded from central Asia, and Babur became emperor in 1526. After two centuries of splendor, Mogul power declined during the eighteenth century, while Britain grew progressively more powerful in the region. The last emperor, Bahadur Shah II, was dethroned by the British in 1858 for his part in the 1857 rebellion (the "Indian Mutiny").

- Korea's Yi dynasty ruled from 1392 until Japan annexed (took over) the country in 1910.

- The Konbaung dynasty of Burma (now Myanmar) reigned from 1752. The British dethroned the last king, Thibaw, in 1885.

- The present Thai dynasty dates from 1782.

- Laos was an ancient kingdom. Its last dynasty reigned from 1904 until the communist takeover in 1975.

- Vietnam's ruling dynasty (from 1802) ended in 1945, when Emperor Bao Dai abdicated in favor of what he vainly hoped would avoid civil war and achieve a "democratic republican government."

CHAPTER FIVE

THE FUTURE OF MONARCHY

In the past, monarchies appeared wherever settled communities and town life developed. Myths and folktales described the exploits of hero-kings and evil tyrants. The fortunes of nations and peoples were often directly tied to dynasties as they rose and fell. Clearly, monarchy has been an institution of central importance. From the nineteenth century onward, however, societies were transformed with amazing speed by new ideas and new technologies. By the early twenty-first century, some people were questioning whether monarchy had any further role to play.

There are now only a handful of absolute or politically powerful monarchies. These exist in countries where custom and tradition remain strong and change has been slow. The outside world has already made an impact through technologies like television, computers, the Internet, and mobile phones. This impact seems likely to grow stronger as large numbers of people become educated and prosperous and expect to have a voice in the way their country is run.

In the twenty-first century, the remaining absolute monarchies seem likely to yield to the now almost universal belief that governments should be chosen by the people and answerable to them—in other words, to the democratic spirit.

Constitutional monarchies appear to have much better prospects. They have worked well in countries where peaceful changes of government take place according to recognized rules. In these circumstances, the monarch can play a

Queen Elizabeth II is greeted by a host of Union flags on a visit to Aylesbury, Buckinghamshire, UK, in May 2002. Whatever the standing of other "royals," she remains popular and respected. ▶

nonpolitical role without difficulty. Monarchies are more vulnerable when there are upheavals, as happened in Greece in 1967, costing Constantine II his throne.

Even in some politically stable constitutional monarchies, however, republicanism made some headway in the 1990s. Problems within Britain's royal family (*see page 41*) raised doubts about their role, and one respected newspaper, the *Guardian*, declared itself in favor of a republic. During the same period, a strong republican movement developed in Australia but failed in its bid to abolish the monarchy.

THE REPUBLICAN ARGUMENT

Most republicans do not oppose monarchy simply because of the way individual monarchs behave. They believe that monarchy, including constitutional monarchy, is wrong in principle, based as it is

> *"Those who imagine that a politician would make a better figurehead than a hereditary monarch might perhaps make the acquaintance of more politicians."*
>
> Baroness Margaret Thatcher, herself a politician (British prime minister 1979–1990), in a speech made in 1985.

on the idea that "royal blood" is something special. Clearly monarchs are only special beings in so far as they have been shaped by lives of privilege and wealth. Almost everybody now agrees that a person's position in the world should be based on factors such as work, talent, and achievement. Yet monarchs and royal families owe their position entirely to accidents of birth.

The existence of the monarchy also helps to maintain an undesirable division of society into ranks (dukes, earls, barons, and other titles), similarly based on birth. Even the language of monarchy is seen by many as degrading to a free people,

REPUBLICANISM IN AUSTRALIA

Queen Elizabeth II of Great Britain is also Queen of Australia. She is represented by a governor-general (and by governors of the individual states that make up Australia). Although Australians choose these officers, discontent with the monarchy has grown. In 1991, the Labour Party, then in power, came out in favor of a republic, and opinion polls consistently showed a majority of Australians agreeing. Republicans argued that a non-resident head of state could not adequately represent the country. They said that Australia was no longer mainly "British" in outlook and that monarchy conflicted with Australian beliefs in social and sexual equality. Campaigning on the issue was confused, with republicans divided about exactly what kind of head of state they wanted. Possibly for this reason, 55 percent of voters favored keeping the monarchy. The vote against monarchy was large, and opinion polls continued to be pro-republican. Nevertheless, with a conservative prime minister, John Howard, who was "an unashamed royalist," the issue appears to have been shelved.

UNLUCKY DYNASTY

India is one of several republics in which a single family has behaved very like a royal dynasty. Jawaharlal Nehru was a leading figure in the Indian struggle for independence from Britain. When independence was achieved in 1947, Nehru served as prime minister of India until his death in 1964. After only two years, Nehru's daughter, Mrs. Indira Gandhi, began a long reign as prime minister (1966–77, 1980–84). Her son Sanjay was expected to succeed her, but after his death in an air crash, another son, Rajiv, was brought into politics. When Mrs. Gandhi was assassinated in 1984, Rajiv became prime minister (1984–89). In 1991, while out of power, he too was assassinated. The magic of the "dynasty" was so strong that, in 1998, Rajiv's Italian-born wife Sonia was persuaded to lead the Gandhis' political party, Congress. It won the 2004 general election, although Sonia Gandhi refused to become prime minister.

who are called "subjects," not "citizens" as in a republic. The monarch is often linked with a state religion, although most societies increasingly have people of many faiths and also the non-religious. In these ways, monarchies seem to encourage an out-of-date view of society.

THE MONARCHIST ARGUMENT

Defenders of constitutional monarchies deny most of this. They claim that such arguments are based on abstract ideas rather than realities. They emphasize the importance of tradition in holding societies together. They also believe that when ordinary people express feelings of intense emotional loyalty toward royalty, this response is perfectly natural and patriotic.

Monarchists may also argue that, in the real world, emotions are still focused on human leaders. In fact, support for dynasties is such a natural development that it often appears, unofficially,

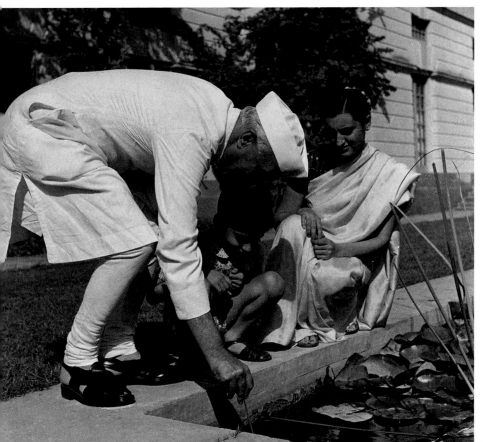

India's ruling political "dynasty" in 1950: Prime Minister Jawaharlal Nehru with his daughter Indira Gandhi and her son Rajiv, both future prime ministers.

PERILS OF KINGSHIP

The Greek monarchy was the most recent European monarchy to fall. In April 1967, a group of army officers seized power. "The Colonels," as they soon became known, abolished Greek democracy but did not interfere with the monarchy. Then, in December 1967, King Constantine II attempted to overthrow the Colonels. He failed to rally the army behind him and fled to Italy. The Colonels lost power in 1973, but the Greeks voted for a republic and Constantine remained in exile.

"The State functions more easily if it can be personified. An elected President who has stepped out of politics ... is no substitute for a King who has stepped in by right of inheritance. Still less is an active politician, like the President of the United States, a substitute. We can damn the Government and cheer the King."

W. Ivor Jennings in his book, *The British Constitution*, first published in 1943.

in republics. Three generations of the Nehru-Gandhi family governed India, with hardly a break, from 1947. The Kennedy and Bush families have been remarkably prominent in U.S. political life. More than one woman has become president or prime minister of a country by being chosen to follow her husband in office, as if he were a hereditary monarch.

All of this suggests that the stability and continuity offered by a monarchy remains of importance to many in a democratic society. Governments may go through crises or become paralyzed, but the monarchical head of state is always on duty. The hereditary succession ensures that there is no break between sovereigns and no dispute as to who should take on the office. Constitutional monarchs have no links with any elected political party, so people with all sorts of views can feel loyalty toward them. Key groups such as the armed forces, the police, and the civil service benefit from feeling that, although they obey each government as it takes office, their final loyalty is to the crown,

▲ U.S. president John F. Kennedy poses for the press with his wife Jackie and their children on Easter 1963. The Kennedys were often described as the United States' "royal family."

King Christian X of Denmark is seen here in 1920, entering southern Jutland in triumph after the area voted to become part of Denmark. Later, the king and his white horse became symbols of Danish resistance to Nazi rule. ▶

ROYAL COMEBACK

In 1989–1990, the communist regimes of Eastern Europe collapsed. Democracies were set up in their place, and it was sometimes suggested that monarchies might be re-established in countries such as Russia and Romania. So far the only real comeback has been in Bulgaria. In 1946, the communists abolished the monarchy and nine-year-old King Simeon II went into exile. Following the communist collapse, Simeon, now a successful businessman, was able to revisit Bulgaria. In 2001, he settled there permanently and organized a political party, the National Movement. In June 2001, it won a general election, and the ex-king became prime minister of Bulgaria, no longer Simeon II but using his family name, Simeon Borisov Sakskoburggotski.

(rather than to an abstract "nation") and through the crown to the people. In this way, the monarch symbolizes the nation and embodies its past glories and present unity.

This unifying role may be particularly important in states where there are several groups with separate national traditions, for example in Britain (English, Welsh, Scottish, and Irish) and in Belgium (Walloons and Flemings). It is arguably more natural to feel an intense attachment to human beings than to an abstraction such as "the republic." Admirers of monarchy often refer to this nation-rallying role of the British royal family in World War II, when the country was being ravaged by German bombing. During the same conflict, Denmark's King Christian X set an example for his people after Nazi Germany conquered his country. He encouraged support of Danish Jews and non-cooperation with the Nazis, who eventually imprisoned him.

Monarchists also point out what they claim to be the weaknesses of a republican alternative. In a republic, the head of state is usually a president, who may be a powerful figure, as in the United States, or a figurehead, resembling an elected version of a constitutional monarch, as in Germany. In either case, he or she will stand for a political party or viewpoint opposed by many and will not represent the entire country. Where people distrust politicians, such a head of state may not arouse much enthusiasm.

Republicans, of course, disagree with most of these arguments. For example, they point out that, in the United States and France, republican institutions have not prevented their peoples from being passionately patriotic. The debate goes on. The fate of constitutional monarchies will probably not be decided by discussion, however, but by the popularity of royal individuals and families.

MODELS OR CELEBRITIES?

Constitutional monarchies have chosen to adapt themselves to the great social changes of the past century. In 1900, monarchs were splendid, bemedaled and bejeweled figures, remote from the mass of the people. In the course of the twentieth century, this side of monarchy was maintained on great state occasions, but royal families increasingly took on a more "ordinary" image. They frequently appeared in everyday clothing and had more contact with their subjects through activities such as visiting factories and attending sporting events. The monarchies

UNEQUAL PARTNERS

Only one person normally inherits a throne. The husband or wife of that person is known as his, or her, consort. Confusingly, both a female monarch who reigns in her own right and the wife of a king may be called a queen. The husband of a reigning queen, however, is not called a king. Perhaps the best-known male royal consort was Queen Victoria's husband, "the Prince Consort," Prince Albert (lived 1819–1861), who played a prominent part in British life. More recent examples include Prince Bernhard (1911–2004), husband of Queen Juliana of the Netherlands, and Philip, Duke of Edinburgh (born 1921), who is married to Britain's Queen Elizabeth II.

PRINCESS DIANA

Diana, Princess of Wales, was the most famous and popular royal figure of recent times. In 1981, as Lady Diana Spencer, she married the heir to the British throne, Charles, Prince of Wales. Carried to her wedding in a glass coach, she was seen as a "fairy-tale princess" and subsequently brought glamour to many royal occasions. After her marriage to Charles failed, the couple separated in 1992 and were divorced in 1996. Diana remained a prominent figure, campaigning for good causes such as funding for the treatment of the disease AIDS. She was popular because of her warm personal style, expressing emotion and making physical contact, which contrasted with the normal, stiffly dignified royal manner. Well-publicized personal difficulties and love affairs did not dent her popularity. In 1997, 36-year-old Diana and her companion, Dodi Fayed, were killed when their car crashed in Paris. Her death prompted a worldwide outpouring of grief and sympathy and, in Britain, criticism of the royal family's initially cool response. Whether the monarchy would suffer any long-term effects is as yet unclear.

▲ Princess Diana (pictured here in 1997) was wife of Charles, Prince of Wales. At once glamorous and apparently "ordinary," she was much admired. The royal family's popularity suffered when they were rumored to have treated her badly.

Edward VIII in March 1936, making his first radio broadcast as king. In December, he broadcast again to tell the British nation he would abdicate.

of the Netherlands and Scandinavia cultivated this "ordinary" image most thoroughly, but the British and other European monarchies were also affected by the trend.

The ordinariness of royal families, however, is of an idealized, unblemished kind. They are—or are presented as—model families, happy and united. They are held up as an example to their peoples. In Britain, this was true of the family lives of George V (r. 1910–1936), George VI (r. 1936–1952), and Elizabeth II (r. 1952–). The standards they upheld were actually higher than those of ordinary people. By 1936, divorce was becoming acceptable, but when King Edward VIII insisted on marrying an American divorcée named Wallis Simpson, he was forced to abdicate after reigning for less than a year. Even in 1955, Queen Elizabeth's sister, Princess Margaret,

BELGIAN BREAKS

Normally, the moment a monarch dies, the reign of the next monarch begins. Present-day Belgium is an exception. There, the would-be king or queen must take an oath to the constitution before he or she can take office. This means that there are brief gaps between the reigns of Belgian monarchs.

experienced similar pressures and gave up the idea of marrying a divorced man.

In the next few decades, standards changed very rapidly. Younger members of royal families were influenced by new social trends and more often made personal choices (especially of marriage partners) that conflicted with traditional behavior.

At the same time, the lives of royal individuals were investigated and described at length by newspapers, television, and other media. In the past, the media had presented royalty in the most favorable light, often suppressing any unwelcome facts. Changing that, late twentieth-century journalists, equipped with tape recorders and zoom-lens cameras, fed the public with accounts of royal lapses, love affairs, quarrels, and divorces.

A modern image of monarchy: Prince William, grandson of Queen Elizabeth II, is shown casually dressed and kicking a ball on a beach in Scotland in 2003. ▶

The immediate effect was largely to destroy the perfect-family image of royalty. People who had idealized royal families were disillusioned. All that had happened, in fact, was that royalty were seen to have the same problems as other people; this did not necessarily make them unpopular. In fact, royalty seemed to be becoming part of present-day "celebrity culture," like film stars whose escapades are followed by millions of people. So it is possible that royalty will settle into a new public role. Alternatively, more effective measures may be taken to safeguard the privacy of "royals" and to influence the way they are perceived by the public.

It is clearly too soon to know how such developments will affect the governmental system of monarchy. Over the centuries, it has proven flexible enough to take on widely different roles, so it may well continue to find an important place in the rapidly changing modern world.

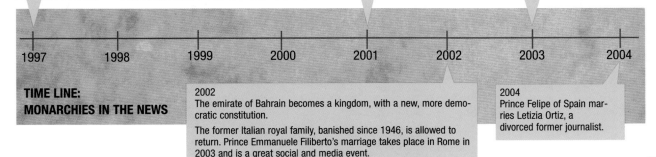

1997
Diana, Princess of Wales, is killed in a car crash.

2001
Norway's Crown Prince marries a single mother and former waitress; popular interest is great.

During an argument, the Crown Prince of Nepal shoots the king and several other members of his family, then kills himself.

Ex-king Simeon II is elected prime minister of his former kingdom, Bulgaria.

2003
Electors in Liechtenstein vote to give the prince greatly extended powers.

Protests force King Mswati III of poverty-stricken Swaziland to give up plans to buy an executive jet.

1997   1998   1999   2000   2001   2002   2003   2004

TIME LINE: MONARCHIES IN THE NEWS

2002
The emirate of Bahrain becomes a kingdom, with a new, more democratic constitution.

The former Italian royal family, banished since 1946, is allowed to return. Prince Emmanuele Filiberto's marriage takes place in Rome in 2003 and is a great social and media event.

2004
Prince Felipe of Spain marries Letizia Ortiz, a divorced former journalist.

TIME LINE

3000 B.C.E.	THE FIRST CIVILIZATIONS APPEAR IN EGYPT AND MESOPOTAMIA, RULED BY MONARCHS.
C.1600 B.C.E.	MYCENAEAN KINGDOMS APPEAR IN GREECE.
1479 B.C.E.	HATSHEPSUT, THE FIRST KNOWN FEMALE RULER IN HISTORY, TAKES POWER IN EGYPT.
510 B.C.E.	THE KINGS OF ROME ARE DRIVEN OUT.
325 B.C.E.	ALEXANDER THE GREAT CONQUERS A VAST EMPIRE.
221 B.C.E.	CHINESE EMPIRE IS FOUNDED.
C.40 B.C.E.	JIMMU, LEGENDARY FIRST EMPEROR OF JAPAN.
30 B.C.E.	DEATH OF CLEOPATRA, LAST QUEEN OF EGYPT; AUGUSTUS BECOMES, IN EFFECT, THE FIRST ROMAN EMPEROR.
C.E. 476	END OF THE ROMAN EMPIRE IN THE WEST.
632—740	ARABS CONQUER VAST AREAS OF THE MIDDLE EAST AND NORTH AFRICA; CALIPHATE FOUNDED
800	CHARLEMAGNE CROWNED EMPEROR IN ROME.
893	OLEG BECOMES THE FIRST KNOWN RUSSIAN RULER AS PRINCE OF KIEV.
1014—1035	KING CNUT RULES DENMARK, NORWAY, AND ENGLAND.
1206—1227	GENGHIS KHAN FOUNDS MONGOL EMPIRE.
1438	A HABSBURG BECOMES HOLY ROMAN EMPEROR; THE OFFICE IS ALMOST ALWAYS HELD BY THE HABSBURG FAMILY UNTIL 1806.
1485—1603	TUDOR DYNASTY CREATES STRONG ENGLISH MONARCHY; MONARCHS INCLUDE HENRY VIII (R.1509—1547) AND ELIZABETH I (R.1558—1603).
1500—1600	"NEW MONARCHIES" EMERGE IN EUROPE.
1521—1533	SPANIARDS OVERTHROW THE AZTEC AND INCA EMPIRES.
1526	MOGULS FOUND AN EMPIRE IN INDIA; IT LASTS UNTIL 1858.
1533	MICHAEL ROMANOV FOUNDS THE DYNASTY THAT RULES RUSSIA UNTIL 1917.
1556—1621	UNDER PHILIP II (R.1556—1598) AND PHILIP III (R.1598—1621), SPAIN DOMINATES EUROPE.

1643–1715	LOUIS XIV REIGNS AS ABSOLUTE RULER UNDER WHOM FRANCE DOMINATES EUROPE.
1649	THE ENGLISH KING CHARLES I IS EXECUTED AFTER LOSING THE CIVIL WARS OF 1642–1649; THE MONARCHY IS RESTORED IN 1660.
1688	IN ENGLAND, THE "GLORIOUS REVOLUTION" OVERTHROWS KING JAMES II; A CONSTITUTIONAL MONARCHY IS SET UP UNDER KING WILLIAM III AND QUEEN MARY.
1783	BRITAIN LOSES THE AMERICAN REVOLUTION AND ITS COLONIES BECOME THE UNITED STATES OF AMERICA.
1789	THE FRENCH REVOLUTION LEADS TO THE EXECUTION OF THE KING (1793) AND THE FOUNDING OF A REPUBLIC.
1805	NAPOLEON BONAPARTE BECOMES EMPEROR OF THE FRENCH; THE MONARCHY IS RESTORED AFTER HIS FALL IN 1815, BUT FRANCE ULTIMATELY BECOMES A REPUBLIC IN 1870.
1815	WILLIAM I OF ORANGE BECOMES FIRST KING OF THE NETHERLANDS.
1830	LEOPOLD I BECOMES FIRST KING OF NEWLY INDEPENDENT BELGIUM.
1910	FALL OF THE PORTUGUESE MONARCHY.
1911	4,000-YEAR-OLD CHINESE EMPIRE IS REPLACED BY A REPUBLIC.
1914–1918	WORLD WAR I LEADS TO THE END OF THE EMPIRES OF RUSSIA (1917), AUSTRIA-HUNGARY (1918), GERMANY (1918), AND TURKEY (1922).
1921	KING SOBHUZA II LIBERATES THE AFRICAN KINGDOM OF SWAZILAND FROM THE BRITISH AND REIGNS UNTIL 1982, WHEN HE IS SUCCEEDED BY HIS SON, KING SOBHUZA II.
1932	KINGDOM OF IBN SAUD BECOMES OFFICIALLY KNOWN AS SAUDI ARABIA.
1939	ALBANIA'S MONARCHY ENDS WHEN THE COUNTRY IS INVADED BY ITALY.
1945–1947	MONARCHIES OF YUGOSLAVIA, ITALY, BULGARIA, AND ROMANIA ARE ABOLISHED.
1952	QUEEN ELIZABETH II COMES TO BRITISH THRONE.
1952–1962	EGYPT, LIBYA, IRAQ, AND YEMEN BECOME REPUBLICS.
1973	GREECE BECOMES A REPUBLIC.
1975	THE SPANISH MONARCHY, ABOLISHED IN 1931, IS RESTORED. JUAN CARLOS I BECOMES KING.
1993	NORODOM SIHANOUK IS RESTORED TO THE CAMBODIAN THRONE.
2002	THE EMIRATE OF BAHRAIN BECOMES A CONSTITUTIONAL MONARCHY.

GLOSSARY

abdicate resign one's crown and allow a successor to take one's place

aristocracy the nobility, usually ranked directly below the monarch

autocracy a political system or state in which an individual ruler is all-powerful

autocrat the ruler in an autocracy

Barbarians uncivilized, usually ferocious people; the Romans used the word, not necessarily fairly, of all peoples outside their empire

caesar title used by Roman emperors; originally the family name of Julius Caesar

Caliphate the lands ruled by the caliph, the supreme political and religious leader during the early centuries of the Islamic empire

city-state relatively small state with a single city at its heart

colonies territories, overseas or abroad, that belong to a state; Canada, for example, was once a British colony

communist describes a political system, bitterly hostile to monarchy, which claimed to create a just society; in practice, communist governments have usually been rigid dictatorships, and most failed by the 1990s

constitution the basic political rules in a society, often set down in a document; it defines how government should operate and how laws should be made

constitutional monarchy political system in which the monarch's powers, rights, and duties are limited and defined by law

coronation the ceremony of crowning the king or queen

czar the name of the ruler in Russia; derives from caesar

democracy political system in which the government and law-makers are elected by all the people

democratic describes a democracy and its operations and outlook

despot all-powerful ruler; the word usually implies that the ruler is unjust or cruel

despotism state ruled bya despot; the actions of a despot

dynasty monarchs belonging to the same family

emir title given to the ruler of some Middle Eastern states

federation a number of states or provinces that have united while while continuing to control their own affairs

Franks a Germanic people; as the Roman Empire declined, the Franks moved into what is now France (originally *Frankia,* land of the Franks)

hereditary inherited

Industrial Revolution major economic advance that involved new forms of power and machinery and mass production techniques; begun in eighteenth-century Britain, it affected the entire globe

insignia objects or badges symbolizing authority

kaiser the name used for ruler in Germany; derives from caesar

khan Mongol title for ruler

Khmer Rouge a communist movement that ruled Cambodia from 1975 to 1979

military dictatorship dictatorship exercised by army leaders

miter a liturgical headress

mogul an Indian Muslim or someone descended from one of several conquering groups of Mongol, Turkish, or Persian origin

Muhammad prophet and founder of the religion of Islam in the seventh century C.E.; Arab followers of this religion militarily conquered vast areas

nomadic wandering; used to describe peoples that graze their flocks by moving from place to place

orb a sphere surmounted by a cross symbolizing kingly power and justice

pharaoh Egyptian ruler

plunder loot: supplies and valuables carried off by soldiers or robbers

propaganda information presented in a biased way, intended to win support for the propagandist or damage an enemy

Reformation reforming religious movement, begun in 1517 by the German monk Martin Luther; his followers, who became known as Protestants, eventually broke away from the Roman Catholic Church to form their own churches

retainers servants or faithful followers, usually of a great lord

Salic Law the exclusion of

females from inheriting the crown

scepter a staff borne by a sovereign as a symbol of authority

shah ruler

shogun a military ruler of Japan

state a general term used in this book because it covers every type of independent political unit (country, nation, federation, empire). Not to be confused with smaller units within some countries that are also called states, such as. the fifty states making up the United States.

sultan the sovereign of a Muslim state

United Nations organization representing the world's nations and often involved in international crises

Visigoths a Germanic people who crossed into the Roman Empire and established a kingdom in Spain

Books

Barton-Wood, Sara. *Queen Elizabeth II.* Hodder Wayland, 2001.

Bernard, Catherine J. *British Empire and Queen Victoria in World History.* Enslow Publishers, 2003.

Chrisp, Peter. *Alexander the Great.* Dorling Kindersley, 2000.

Chrisp, Peter. *The World of the Roman Empire.* Macdonald Young Books, 1999.

Grant, Neil. *Kings and Queens.* Collins, 2003.

Hindley, Geoffrey. *Royal Families of Europe.* Constable, 2000.

Myers, Walter Dean. *At Her Majesty's Request: An African Princess in Victorian England.* Scholastic Press, 1999.

Ross, Stewart. *The Pharaohs.* Hodder Wayland, 2001.

Web Sites

www.canadianheritage.gc.ca/progs/cpsc-ccsp/fr-rf/index_e.cfm

www.factmonster.com/ce6/world/A0856906.html
    members.aol.com/_ht_a/aafri/king.html

www.free-definition.com/monarchy.html

www.monarchyfreecanada.org

www.royal.gov.uk/output/Page1.asp

www.thaiembdc.org/monarchy/monarchy.htm

www.wsu.edu/ ~dee/CIVAFRCA/FOREST.HTM

INDEX